S0-ABB-513

TIMELESS PLACES

PARIS

JUDITH MAHONEY PASTERNAK

MetroBooks

MetroBooks

An Imprint of the Michael Friedman Publishing Group, Inc.

©2000 by Michael Friedman Publishing Group, Inc.
First MetroBooks edition 2002

All rights reserved. No part of this publication may be reproduced, stored in a retrieval system, or transmitted, in any form or by any means, electronic, mechanical, photocopying, recording, or otherwise, without prior written permission from the publisher.

Library of Congress Cataloging-in-Publication Data

Pasternak, Judith Mahoney.
    Paris / Judith Mahoney Pasternak.
        p. cm. — (Timeless places)
    Includes index.
    ISBN 1-58663-883-1
        1. Paris (France)—Civilization. 2. Paris (France)—Pictorial works. I. Title. II. Series.

DC715 .P32 2000
944'.36—dc21

                                                                99-056402

Editor: Ann Kirby-Payne
Art Director: Jeff Batzli
Designer: Jennifer O'Connor
Photography Editor: Erin Feller
Production Managers: Richela Fabian-Morgan and Camille Lee

Color separations by Spectrum Pte. Ltd.
Printed in Hong Kong by Midas Printing Limited

1 3 5 7 9 10 8 6 4 2

For bulk purchases and special sales, please contact:
Michael Friedman Publishing Group, Inc.
Attention: Sales Department
230 Fifth Avenue
New York, NY 10001
212/685-6610 FAX 212/685-3916

Visit our website:
www.metrobooks.com

PAGE 1: **Around the turn of this century, hundreds of new six- and seven-story buildings created what is now the look of residential Paris, with its graceful wrought-iron balconies and gabled roofs.**

PAGES 2-3: **A quiet moment late at night on the Pont St. Michel, usually bustling with students crossing from the Île de la Cité to the gateway of the Latin Quarter at the Place St. Michel.**

PAGES 4-5: **A Greek statue stands watch over the garden surrounding the Chateau of Versailles, a short train ride away from Paris, and yet a perfectly preserved link to a more extravagant past.**

PAGE 6: **Along the Seine, an artist's canvas offers a scene within a scene, capturing the picturesque view from the Left Bank.**

Contents

RIGHT: **The most ornate of the bridges over the Seine, the Pont Alexandre III was built in 1896 at the end of the Gilded Age for the World Exhibition of 1900. A century later it was restored to its original glittering splendor.**

PAGE 10-11: **One of the most charming squares in Paris, the Place des Vosges was planned in the seventeenth century as the central plaza of the city's first luxury apartment complex. In the nineteenth century, the great writer and advocate for democracy Victor Hugo was its most distinguished resident; his apartment is now a museum filled with memorabilia of his turbulent life.**

PART I

L'HISTOIRE

SOUTH OF THE SEINE AND NOTRE DAME, TOWARD THE EASTERN EDGE OF PARIS, THE LEFT BANK RISES STEEPLY FROM THE 213-FOOT (65M) HILL CALLED THE MONTAGNE STE. GENEVIÈVE, CROWNED BY THE IMMENSE EIGHTEENTH-CENTURY PANTHÉON. FROM THERE THE MONTAGNE FALLS AWAY INTO ONE OF THE CITY'S MOST CHARMING NEIGHBORHOODS, THE CONTRESCARPE-MOUFFETARD QUARTER.

IF ON A GRAY MORNING YOU SHOULD ZIG-ZAG THROUGH AND AROUND THE QUARTER, STARTING ALONG THE STOLID RUE MONGE, YOU'LL COME TO THE ARÈNES DE LUTÈCE, THE ROMAN ARENA BUILT WHEN THE CITY WAS CALLED LUTETIA, AND STILL IN USE TODAY. THEN, IF YOU WALK UP THE HILL TO THE CORNER OF THE RUE ST. JACQUES AND THE RUE SOUFFLOT, YOU'LL SEE AHEAD OF YOU, JUST ACROSS THE SEINE, THE FIFTEENTH-CENTURY TOUR ST. JACQUES RISING OUT OF THE MISTS OF THE RIVER. ON YOUR RIGHT IS THE GREAT DOME OF THE PANTHÉON; A MILE (1.6KM) AWAY ON YOUR LEFT, TOWERING OVER THE MISTS, THE EIFFEL TOWER; AND BEHIND YOU, THE ARÈNES DE LUTÈCE. YOU ARE TRULY AT THE CORNER OF THE CENTURIES.

YOU ARE ALSO AT THE CORNER OF TODAY AND TOMORROW. FOR MORE THAN ANY OTHER CITY OF THE WESTERN WORLD, PARIS IS BOTH A CITY OF YESTERDAY AND A CITY OF *NOW*, TIMELESS RATHER THAN FROZEN IN TIME. AS YOU LOOK, AWESTRUCK, AT THE HISTORY SURROUNDING YOU, YOU STAND AMID THE BUSTLE OF THE STUDENTS OF THE SORBONNE AND

❦

In 1758, Louis XV commissioned Jacques-Germain Soufflot to design a grand new church to honor Ste. Geneviève, the patron saint of Paris. The church, with its great dome, was finished in 1789; the revolutionary government promptly deconsecrated it and renamed it the Panthéon.

The City of Yesterday

the Collège de France. These ancient universities helped make the city famous for its intellectual prowess—and notorious for its bohemian morals. *La vie bohème*; France's gourmet cuisine; and the staggering beauty of streets, river, buildings, and parks all combine to make Paris an icon of sensuality as well as intellect.

The students also brought another quality that came to typify Paris. From the fourteenth century on, they poured in from across Europe, giving the city its quintessentially cosmopolitan air. By the eighteenth century, with Paris the capital of a world empire, its citizens were arriving from across the globe; when the European colonies dissolved in the mid-twentieth century, the former French colonies in Africa and Asia added whole communities to the Paris mix.

Today, with a population of more than two million, Paris has performed the extraordinary feat of preserving the legacy of the ages while adapting itself to the twenty-first century with such hyper-modern structures as the Centre Pompidou museum complex, the Opera Bastille, the Bibliothèque Nationale, and the high-rise business center of La Défense. Its people come from every continent, all of them living and working in a city that is at once a city of the mind and of the senses—and a city of yesterday and today.

Paris has been a city for so long—almost two millennia—that to stroll anywhere in it is to walk through the living text for Western Civilization 101. The pages are deliriously out of order: on one block is the rise and fall of Rome, while just around the corner are the triumphs and tragedies of World War II. So steeped in history is the city that many individual sites contain relics that come from eras centuries apart, for virtually everything that has happened in the West since the beginning of the Common Era has left a marker somewhere on these streets. You don't need to search for clues; they come to meet you as you walk.

Just the same, the details of the founding of the city itself have passed from view. It happened in the middle of the Seine, in the third century B.C.E.: a Celtic tribe the Romans named the Parisii settled on the island now called the Île de la Cité. It was a wonderful place for a settlement. The wide Seine (wider then than it is now) provided both sustenance and protection; its waters were potable and sweet, and marshland stretched away from either bank,

The students at the Sorbonne include both men and women now, their studies covering all subjects. But for its first centuries, the university was only for men studying for the clergy—in Latin, of course, which gave the name "Latin Quarter" to what is now Paris' Fifth Arrondissement.

making anything—or anyone—approaching the island visible from a long way away. But two hundred years later, the Parisii were no match for the technology of imperial Rome. In 52 C.E., the Roman Empire built a provincial Gallic capital they called Lutetia among the hills south of the Seine and on the Île de la Cité.

All traces of the Parisii settlement are gone, but the Left Bank still holds remnants of Lutetia. The few long, straight avenues that connect the narrow, twisting streets—like the Rue St. Jacques—follow the route of the ancient Roman roads, and two of Lutetia's public buildings are still extant. The fifteenth-century Hôtel de Cluny on the Boulevard St. Michel (which now holds the Cluny Museum of medieval arts and crafts) was built upon the ruins of the Roman baths, which remain visible from the boulevard. Further down the Left Bank, almost hidden inside a park that runs along the Rue Monge, its entrance marked by an inconspicuous plaque, is the Arènes de Lutèce, the Roman arena. It isn't even a ruin; the arena has been rebuilt and remains in use to this day. It is one of the places where Parisian men play—and gamble on—

pétanque, a French game similar to Italy's bocce and Scotland's bowls.

With the decline of the Empire, Rome's provincial government abandoned Lutetia. During the early Middle Ages, Europe—including the Frankish city that took the name "Paris" in the fourth century—was assailed by marauding barbarians. In the fifth century, Attila and his Huns stood at the gates of Paris but were turned aside because of the prayers of a pious young Christian named Geneviève. Geneviève subsequently converted Clovis I, king of the Franks, to Christianity, and when she died, she was buried in a church at the top of the Left Bank's highest hill. She was later made a saint. After her canonization, she became revered as the patron saint of Paris, and the hill where she was buried was named the Montagne Ste. Geneviève in her honor.

During the course of the Middle Ages, the city became one of the most important in Europe, the home of one great Gothic church after another. On the Left Bank, the Church of St. Germain des Prés still has its eleventh-century chancel and nave, though the rest of the building was reconstructed

Far from the city center, Montmarte was once a suburb. Its semi-rural nature is still evident in the former name of this café: an *auberge* was a country inn.

during the twelfth and seventeenth centuries. Nearer the Seine, the small Church of St. Julien le Pauvre was built between 1165 and 1220. It was around this time that the great Gothic masterpiece across the left channel of the river, on the Île de la Cité, was built: the Cathedral of Notre Dame. Begun in 1163 and finished in 1345, the Cathedral of Notre Dame is renowned across the globe as one of the most beautiful buildings ever erected.

By the thirteenth century, Paris was one of Europe's major centers of learning. That was when the Sorbonne was founded, the university that gave the Latin Quarter its name. (At the time, all schools were seminaries, and the students studying for the clergy spoke and studied in Latin.) The same century saw the construction of two churches still standing in central Paris: St. Severin on the Left Bank, now in the middle of a pedestrian-only area of inexpensive restaurants, and the exquisite stained-glass wonder that is the other gem of the Île de la Cité, Ste. Chapelle. The latter is now hidden inside the Palais de Justice, where the Parisian courts are headquartered. Curiously, visitors to Ste. Chapelle must take a tour of the courts to reach it.

Yet for all those centuries Paris was not, properly speaking, a major European capital, for there was no French nation for it to be the capital of. Not until the Renaissance, early in the fifteenth century, did the Île de France and the provinces surrounding it—Burgundy, Brittany, and so on—free themselves from the domination of England and constitute the nation of France under the leadership of Jeanne d'Arc, St. Joan, a young peasant leader from Lorraine. It was then that Paris blossomed into a major capital of the Western world, a

bloom that has lasted for five centuries and shows no signs of withering. It was then, too, that the city began to take the shape of the Paris we know today.

Many of the major structures of the fifteenth and sixteenth centuries were built on the Left Bank or toward the eastern end of the Right Bank, in the part of Paris still called the Marais. *Marais* is French for "marsh," and it was during this period that the marshland east of the city was reclaimed. Much of the western section of the Marais was torn down in the early 1980s to make room for the Centre Pompidou, but immediately next to that ultra-modern edifice the sixteenth-century Church of St. Merri, a Renaissance gem begun in 1520, still stands. In 1530, it occurred to King François I that a national university that taught only in Latin was a trifle old-fashioned, and he decided to create a parallel institution that would teach in French. Thus was born the Collège de France, on the Left Bank alongside the Sorbonne. (François also rebuilt the Louvre, the fourteenth-century palace of Charles V, but his efforts would be superseded in the seventeenth century by Louis XIV's much grander reconstruction.) And in 1533, to consolidate the city's administration, work was begun on a City Hall for Paris, the Hôtel de Ville, in the great square called the Place de Grève (site of important municipal events, including executions). It was finished in 1628, by which time it had grown into an immense, flamboyant example of Baroque architecture.

In the sixteenth and seventeenth centuries, a series of religious wars was tearing the new nation apart; when they subsided early in the seventeenth century, an astonishing decade-long surge of development created many of the sights with which all visitors to Paris are still familiar. King Henri IV, the liberal-minded Protestant who to gain the French throne converted to Catholicism (with the quip, "Paris is worth a mass"), nevertheless saw much room for improvement in the city. In 1604, Henri commissioned the construction of a new stone bridge over the Seine, still called the Pont Neuf—the New Bridge—though it is now the oldest one spanning the river. A year later he undertook a more ambitious project, the creation in the reclaimed Marais of the first planned housing project in Paris, a set of apartment buildings surrounding the city's first planned square, the Place des Vosges.

After Henri's assassination in 1610, the completion of the Place des Vosges was overseen by his son, Louis XIII. Henri's widow, Marie de Médicis, unwilling to remain in the Louvre with her son, had a palace modeled on Florence's Pitti Palace built for herself on the Left Bank. The Luxembourg Palace, as it came to be known, now houses the French Senate, and the gardens surrounding it are one of Paris' loveliest parks.

Two centuries after achieving nationhood, France was becoming ever richer and more powerful. Its public buildings followed suit. Louis XIV, the Sun King, built some of the most monumental structures of the seventeenth century. Outside Paris, he turned a rural royal residence into the still-unequaled palace of Versailles. Within the confines of Paris itself, he commissioned the reconstruction of the Louvre into the monumental building we know today. His rule also brought

about the construction of Les Invalides, a huge home and hospital for the veterans of his many wars.

In 1758, his great-grandson, Louis XV, began the rebuilding of the Church of Ste. Geneviève, which would include a dome that would one day dominate the Left Bank skyline. But

In the mid-seventeenth century, Louis XIV turned Versailles, once little more than a royal hunting lodge, into the grandest palace in Europe, surrounded by acre upon acre of formal gardens and wooded groves, each with its own fountain.

the reconstruction was not finished until 1789—just in time to be deconsecrated in the wake of the Revolution. It was renamed the Panthéon, the temple of all the gods.

It was in Paris, of course, that the need for radical change exploded into the conflagration that would sweep all before it and change the face of Europe. France was in dire straits in 1789: its economy was a shambles, the poor were starving, and the emerging middle classes were hardly better off. Only the ancient nobility flourished, its historic privileges intact. In May of that year, Louis XVI convened an Estates Général—a parliament—in Versailles in the hope that the body could enact sufficient reforms to ward off popular unrest. But no reforms could have saved the sinking ship that was the *ancien régime.*

In June, the Third Estate of the Estates Général—the group that represented the people of France (the First and Second Estates represented aristocracy and church, respectively)—reconstituted itself as a National Assembly, with the support of sympathizers among the nobility and the

A symbol of Paris since 1836, the massive Arc de Triomphe is sculpted from ground level to its 164-foot (50m) top with celebrations of France's and Napoleon's military might. Underneath it rests the eternally lit grave of France's unknown soldier.

clergy. Although the king eventually acknowledged the Assembly, his dismissal of his popular and reform-minded finance minister, Jacques Necker, provided the fatal spark. On July 14, 1789, the people of Paris stormed and took the old royal prison, a castle called the Bastille. The rest of the Revolution would play itself out largely in Paris, as the Girondists, the moderate republicans, and the extremist Jacobins fought each other, aristocratic counterrevolutionaires within and outside of the country, and, eventually, other countries for the future of France.

The most famous symbols of the Revolution, the Bastille and the guillotine, are gone now. France abolished capital punishment in 1981, and the Bastille was torn down shortly after it was taken in 1789. At its site, the Place de la Bastille, now stands the 171-foot (52m) Colonne de Juillet (July Column) commemorating the second and third revolutions—those of 1830 and 1848—with the ringing inscription "Liberté, Egalité et Fraternité."

Before the subsequent revolutions, however, came the man who was at once the heir and destroyer of the first one. In 1806, seven years after Napoleon Bonaparte came to power and two years after his coronation as emperor, he commissioned yet another monument that has become an emblem of Paris, the mighty Arc de Triomphe (it stands 164 feet [50m] high) in the Place d'Etoile. Napoleon said the arch was to be a tribute to the French fighting forces that were conquering Europe; presumably, however, he also knew that the triumphal arches of Rome had been raised to the leaders—and emperors—who had fought at the head of the fighting forces. By 1836, when it was finished, Napoleon was long gone, defeated at Waterloo in 1815 and then exiled to St. Helena, where he died in 1821. After a number of relocations, his body was finally laid to rest in 1840 in the Invalides, where it remains today.

For much of the rest of the century, France would alternate among monarchy, empire, and republic (it was then the only republic in Europe). Amazingly, it grew increasingly powerful, laying the foundations of the modern capital. After the fall of Napoleon, the monarchy was restored in the person of Louis XVIII, who was succeeded in 1824 by his brother, Charles X. But republican fervor still flourished in France, and Charles felt forced to institute measures so repressive that he was overthrown in 1830 in favor of the more liberal Louis Philippe. It was in 1833, under Louis Philippe—the last king to rule France—that the oldest monument in Paris was erected—the 3,300-year-old Egyptian obelisk that dominates the Place de la Concorde. It had been a gift from the Viceroy of Egypt to Charles X, but transporting the 220-ton (224t) obelisk proved so difficult that by the time it reached Paris, Charles had been succeeded by Louis Philippe.

The restored monarchy lasted thirty-three years, until its final fall and the proclamation of the Second Republic in 1848, a year of unrest throughout Europe. Under the Second Republic, all men over twenty-one years old could vote, but working people wanted more, and in June 1848, another revolution was brutally suppressed and suffrage narrowed. The Republic lasted four years, until Napoleon's nephew assumed power in 1852 as Napoleon III, head of the Second Empire.

Under Napoleon III's eighteen-year regime, Baron Georges Haussmann, commissioned to plan the city, undertook a series of sweeping constructions and reconstructions: the market-place at Les Halles (now replaced by central Paris' major mall), the great railroad stations (including the Gare d'Orsay, now a museum of nineteenth-century art), and the parks. Haussmann is remembered today for his two greatest achievements, one underground, one above: the reconstruction of the Parisian sewer system (which tourists can still visit), and the grand sweeping boulevards that characterize the city (but were, in fact, created to make it more difficult for rebels to barricade the streets). It was also under Haussmann that the city was divided into the twenty *arrondissements* ("wards" or "zones") that still organize it today.

In 1870, disaster struck France in the form of the Franco-Prussian War. Incredibly, France lost. When Napoleon III was captured at Sedan, the French people retook their govern-ment, declaring the Third Republic on September 4, 1870. But that winter the Prussians besieged Paris and, for the first time since the Romans, a conquering army entered the city. The 1871 Treaty of Versailles ended the occupation and the war (and established the German Empire), but Paris rose in the rebellion of the Commune. That revolt was defeated in May 1871 by soldiers returning from the war. The wall against which the last of the Communards were shot is now the Mur des Fédéristes in Cimetière Père Lachaise.

The Republic endured, but Paris would be occupied by German forces one more time, during World War II. Though the Germans took care to preserve the world's loveliest city, the occupation is still vividly commemorated all across Paris. In every quarter, almost as ubiquitous as the Parisian street signs—and easier to see—are the bronze plaques on buildings that say, "Here fell [a hero's name], fighting for France." Behind Notre Dame, a stunning Memorial to the Martyrs of the Deportation lists all the Third Reich's concentration camps—Auschwitz, Bergen-Belsen, Maidenek, and so on. Iron bars give visitors the chilling sense of imprisonment and doom. At Père Lachaise, too, monuments to victims of each of the camps—and to the Communists, Jews, and other Resistance fighters—memorialize that terrible period. For Paris, "history" is not only what happened a thousand years ago; history is as recent as yesterday.

A City of the Mind

For all the centuries that Paris helped shape the history of the modern world, it was also shaping Western culture. The city has been a leading light of the worlds of art and literature since the founding of the Sorbonne drew students and teachers to Paris from all over Europe in the thirteenth century. So profound and far-reaching have been the cross-currents between the city's political and cultural lives that visions of historical Paris abound in Western literature, and strollers in the city encounter both the people of the past and the characters brought to life by the city's great writers. These writers knew the city well. Most of them lived there, some native, others drawn by the rich intel-lectual life that has characterized Paris for centuries—and by its legendary tolerance for unconventional behavior. Any stroll through Parisian streets follows in the footsteps of scores of bohemian writers and artists of the last five hundred years. So palpable, indeed, is their presence here that generations have drawn inspiration from—and often incorporated into their work—the lives and stories of previous generations.

The giant of French literature, Victor Hugo, for example, left traces all over Paris. His one-time apartment off the Place des Vosges in the Marais is now a museum; his body is buried in the Panthéon; his family lies in Père Lachaise cemetery. Hugo modeled the character Pierre Gringoire in *Notre Dame de Paris* on the fifteenth-century Parisian poet (and, almost certainly, criminal) François Villon. Hugo's placement of the Villonesque Gringoire in the novel is a bit of poetic license;

Open late every evening, the English-language bookstore Shakespeare and Co. on the Left Bank has been a home away from home for American visitors and expatriates for over three incarnations and eight decades.

Villon, who was the author of the one of the most famous lines of French poetry—"Where are the snows of yester-year?"—was almost certainly dead by 1482, the year *Notre Dame de Paris* takes place.

The nineteenth-century Symbolist poets were also centered in Paris. Charles Baudelaire, the poet of *Les Fleurs du Mal* ("Flowers of Evil"), was part of a vibrant circle of poets and painters in Paris. His followers Paul Verlaine and Arthur Rimbaud conducted much of their ill-starred romance in Paris (although it was in Brussels that Verlaine shot Rimbaud in the wrist when the younger man threatened to leave him, ending their love affair once and for all). The building in which Verlaine died on the Left Bank's Rue Descartes is now a hotel. Thirty years after Verlaine's death, the struggling young American writer Ernest Hemingway kept a room there for writing when he found it difficult to work in the tiny apartment nearby he shared with his wife, Hadley, their baby, and a cat.

By late in the nineteenth century Paris had become the cultural capital of the Western world. To the generations following the Symbolists, Paris was the place to be if you were a writer or an artist—especially if your tastes were deemed unsavory in other parts of the world. The Anglo-Irish playwright and poet Oscar Wilde traveled back and forth across the Channel, living and writing in London but recreating in Paris. In 1895, however, at the height of his fame, he was found guilty of "gross indecency" by an English court and sentenced to two years in prison. It was to France he fled when he was released in 1897, and in Paris that he died in 1900. It is in Paris, too, that he is buried; his monument in Père Lachaise cemetery, by sculptor Jacob Epstein, is visited each year by thousands of Europeans and Americans alike for whom he is a symbol both of gay contributions to Western culture and of the persecution of homosexuals.

As he had been in many areas, Wilde was in the avant-garde of those who recognized Paris as a cultural capital. Early twentieth-century Paris was the era of the expatriates. Most of the writers were drawn to the environs of the Latin Quarter, and today it is easy to follow the expatriate trail all over the Left Bank. The self-proclaimed American

Architect Charles Garnier's fabulously ornate ninety-seven-foot (29.6m) main stairway leading up from the lobby of l'Opéra, far from the hidden passages haunted by the famous Phantom of the Opera.

genius Gertrude Stein arrived in 1904; Alice B. Toklas, the woman who would be her partner for the rest of their lives, arrived three years later. They lived just off the Jardin du Luxembourg at 27 Rue de Fleurus, in what is now the deluxe area west of the Latin Quarter. Although relatively little of Stein's writing was published during her lifetime, her profound influence on both twentieth-century literature and on the arts radiated from the Rue de Fleurus outward in space and time. For two generations, from before World War I until after World War II, she and Toklas conducted one of the most brilliant salons of the era, hosting writers like Hemingway and Sherwood Anderson; painters like Henri Matisse, Pablo Picasso, Marie Laurencin, and Henri Rousseau; and composers like Virgil Thomson. The cultural fertilization that resulted is incalculable. Whole schools and movements were nurtured there: Cubism, for one, and a new, stripped-down English prose for another. As recently as the mid-1980s, culture tourists could ring the bell at 27 Rue de Fleurus, and an elderly tenant would show them Stein and Toklas' atelier. Stein and Toklas, too, are buried in Père Lachaise.

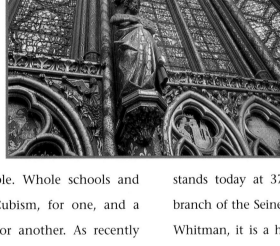

A more modest Left Bank expatriate couple would also exercise an extraordinary influence on twentieth-century literature: Sylvia Beach and her partner, Adrienne Monnier, who founded the English-language bookstore Shakespeare and Co. in 1919 at 8 Rue Dupuytren, near the Ecole de Médecine. Three years later they moved it to 12 Rue de l'Odéon, where it remained for almost twenty years. During that time, Beach and Monnier lent books—for virtually no money— to such struggling Left Bank writers as Ernest Hemingway and James Joyce, allowing them to finish in Paris educations that had been interrupted by the war. The couple's greatest contribution to literature may have been in their recognition of Joyce's genius and their publication of his masterpiece *Ulysses* in 1922 (they also later published sections of *Finnegan's Wake*). A newer incarnation of Shakespeare and Co. stands today at 37 Rue de la Bucherie, just across the left branch of the Seine from Notre Dame. Now owned by George Whitman, it is a haven for a newer generation of struggling American writers, some of whom Whitman allows to stay in an unoccupied room upstairs from the store.

After World War I, the young literati and bohemians flocked to Paris. The young Hemingway—twenty-one at the

The walls of the tiny thirteenth-century Ste. Chapelle, now hidden within the precincts of the Palais de Justice, were executed almost entirely in exquisite stained glass.

time—moved there in 1921 with his bride, Hadley Richardson. They lived at various addresses in and around the Latin Quarter—at one point at 113 Rue Notre Dame des Champs, at another at 74 Rue Cardinal Lemoine. And when they had a child, Hemingway took a room for writing in a hotel where Rue Descartes becomes the Rue Mouffetard. A little later on in the 1920s, Hemingway and his second wife, journalist Pauline Pfeiffer, lived for a time in the Rue Ferou; much later, in 1944, when he had long since left the Left Bank behind along with poverty and obscurity, he would race the victorious U.S. Army into Paris in order to "liberate" Harry's Bar in the Ritz Hotel on the Place Vendôme. But during those first years in Paris, Hemingway was taken under Gertrude Stein's maternal wing. It was she who named Hemingway's generation—young people who had in one way or another lived through World War I—a "lost generation."

These lost ones intended to find themselves in Paris. Many found their talents; more of them found the *vie de bohème*. Hemingway, whose stripped, spare prose changed the way everyone after him wrote the English language, described

their lives street by street, café by café, and drink by drink, both in his fiction—most conspicuously in *The Sun Also Rises*—and in his memoir of those years, *A Moveable Feast*. In the novel, his characters use the cafés clustered near the intersection of the Boulevard Montparnasse and the Boulevard Raspail—the Closerie des Lilas, the Rotonde, the Select—strictly as watering holes. In his memoir, however, he also describes a daytime routine in the same cafés, where he often went to write. Today, the Boulevard Montparnasse has lost some of its glamour, but culture tourists still toast the between-the-wars literati with drinks at the Closerie des Lilas and the Rotonde.

Other "lost generation" writers who made Paris their home between the wars included the doomed F. Scott Fitzgerald; Sherwood Anderson, who wrote in Paris about empty Midwestern American lives; the English chronicler of World War I, Ford Madox Ford; the mad poet Ezra Pound, who later in the decade embraced Italian Fascism and was institutionalized in the United States after World War II; and the American novelist John Dos Passos, whose epic,

Some Parisian artists find their inspiration in the streets and hills of Montmartre, painting from any vantage point where they can find room to set up an easel. Others make their living drawing crayon and pastel portraits of the tourists who come to Montmartre to see the artists at work.

left-leaning novels of American life included the trilogies *U.S.A.* and *The 42nd Parallel*.

Nor was the "lost generation" the last to find a home in Paris. After World War II, a new generation of African-American writers fought their way to publication in the United States. Their task was to describe the realities of the African-American experience, realities they could not themselves escape in their homeland; some, like Richard Wright and James Baldwin, found that Paris was more racially tolerant as well as more tolerant of unconventional lives.

Artists, too, found Paris more congenial to their lives and work than were their hometowns. Impressionism was born there at an exhibition of 1874, when a disdainful critic named a school of painting after a work by Claude Monet. The show also included works by Paul Cézanne, the American painter Alfred Sisley, and Berthe Morisot. If the writers congregated on the Left Bank, generations of painters hung out at the top of the Right Bank, in Montmartre. It was the post-Impressionists—the *fauves*, or wild beasts—who made Montmartre famous at the end of the nineteenth century, especially the disabled portraitist of Paris night life, Henri de Toulouse-Lautrec. A little later, the tragically short-lived Amadeo Modigliani made Montmartre his home.

Still later, Maurice Utrillo, son of the painter Suzanne Valadon, painted a different face of Montmartre life, the outdoor cafés and squares that made it so charming.

It was in Montmartre, too, that Picasso was living when he, his Spanish compatriot Juan Gris, Georges Braque, and Fernand Léger developed Cubism, a profound revolution in modern art, in the early years of the twentieth century. Picasso lived in a studio called the Bateau Lavoir, though he spent much of his social time on the Left Bank at Stein and Toklas' salons. In 1907, the Left and Right Banks met at a legendary banquet held by Picasso's then-lover, Fernande Olivier for the mild-mannered "primitive," Henri Rousseau.

If the post–World War I Left Bank was a hotbed of literary activity, the area became newly famous after World War II for its philosophers. Existentialism made its home in the Latin Quarter, a little to the north of the Hemingway trail, closer to the Sorbonne along the Boulevard St. Michel. The dean of Existentialism, Jean-Paul Sartre, and his lifelong partner, the feminist pioneer Simone de Beauvoir, made les Deux Magots at 170 Boulevard St. Germaine as famous as Hemingway had made the Closerie des Lilas, the Rotonde, and the Select. Sartre and de Beauvoir now rest together at the Cimetière Montparnasse.

Montmartre is famous for its night life. The Place Pigalle is down-at-the-heels now, and the Moulin Rouge immortalized by Toulouse-Lautrec is an overpriced tourist trap, but the Montmartre cafés still lure visitors with the glamor of *la vie bohème*.

Some of Paris' old-fashioned grocery stores have been replaced by supermarkets, but many survive, like this one, specializing in the ultimate delicacies of the Parisian dinner: wines, desserts, and chocolate.

Paris still draws the bohemians of the world. Perhaps the youngest celebrity buried in Père Lachaise is the American poet and rock legend of the 1960s, Jim Morrison. Almost thirty years after his death, a new generation of counter-culturalists still visits his last resting place, and cemetery caretakers periodically have to remove graffiti on other headstones pointing out to visitors (with the word "Jim" and an arrow) the way to his grave.

A City of the Senses

What makes Paris unique is that for its considerable hold on the intellect and the imagination, it is also—sometimes even first of all—a city of the senses. For centuries, it was the West's capital of sensuality, whether a visitor's tastes ran to the pleasures of the palate or naughtier indulgences. At the same time, it has been and remains the capital of romance, a city for lovers and honeymooners—and one of the most beautiful cities in the world.

French cooking is, of course, a byword for gourmet food, and Paris remains the home of four-star dining. But one need not eat at Tour d'Argent or Maxim's to dine gloriously in Paris. Small bistros and cafés by the hundreds serve heavenly multi-course dinners, from *crème de lentilles au foie gras* to *coquilles St. Jacques* to *mousse au chocolat*, for moderate prices.

Nor is dinner the only occasion for gourmet gratification. The "continental" breakfast of bread and coffee may be austere compared to dinner, but when the bread is a freshly baked croissant or brioche, and the coffee is Paris-brewed, the *petit dejeuner* has its own particular pleasure. And at midday, all over Paris, restaurants—be they four-star or neighborhood bistros—serve an abbreviated version of their dinner menu for lunch. Not very abbreviated, however; the Parisian lunch can take hours. Those who don't want to take that much time for lunch eat happily by stopping at a *boulangerie* for a tarte or two, a *pâtisserie* for a dessert, and an *épicerie* for a bottle of water or juice, and enjoy an *al fresco* lunch in a nearby park or place.

And food is only the beginning of the city's sensual delights. The City of Light's nightlife is as legendary as its cuisine. Paris earned its reputation as a city of sin during the eighteenth and nineteenth centuries, when the dream of every well-bred young man from elsewhere in Europe was to have a French mistress. The opera and the theaters that provided the respectable end of the entertainment spectrum also provided women—singers and dancers—who were not quite respectable but who were available. Lower down on the spectrum, the cafés of Montmartre—most notoriously, the Moulin Rouge—provided the earthier entertainment of the can-can, celebrated in the music of Jacques Offenbach and the drawings of Toulouse-Lautrec.

Most people can only eat—or, for that matter, make love—so many times in a day. But the eye has no such limits, and Paris is above all a feast for the eye. The heir of a thousand years of architectural energy and beauty, Paris has extraordinary sights at every turn. It has some of the planet's most exquisite structures, as well as some of the quirkiest—indeed, some of those that seemed peculiar when they were built have come to seem beautiful to succeeding generations.

The list of beauties of Paris begins, of course, with Notre Dame, the grand gothic cathedral in the heart of the city, the queen of churches called by many the loveliest intact building in the world. Notre Dame's astonishing combination of mass and grace, its great towers, and peerless thirty-three-foot (10m) Rose Window have made it one of the glories of France for more than seven centuries.

In the heart of the Right Bank is the grandiose Théâtre National de l'Opéra, planned by Haussman in 1820, designed by Charles Garnier in 1860, and opened in 1875 as the triumph of the Belle Epoque, the Gilded Age. High above the Right Bank in Montmartre is the great white Romano-Byzantine Basilica Sacré Coeur, conceived in 1871 after the Franco-Prussian War, but not finished until 1919. Here and there across the city are the original Art Nouveau entrances to the Métro (the Paris subway) by sculptor Hector Guimard. Finally, of course, there is the Eiffel Tower, visible from almost anywhere in the city. Soaring above the city's southern skyline, the 984-foot (300m) tower (1050 feet [320m] with its television mast) was greeted with equal measures of praise and derision when it was built for the Paris Exposition of 1889. Two decades later, plans were underway to demolish it, but at the last moment a reprieve was granted because of the structure's usefulness as a radiotelegraph antenna. Today, of course, it is known the world over as an emblem of Paris.

Then there are the vistas. Because central Paris has so few high-rise buildings, there are unobstructed views of the city in

A study in contrasts: the centuries-old walls of the Louvre surround the new glass pyramid entrance designed by American architect I.M. Pei.

every quarter. In every direction something wonderful rises over picturesquely twisting streets or down grand boulevards: Notre Dame in the center, the Eiffel Tower to the south, Sacré Coeur to the north, the Obelisk of Luxor and the Arc de Triomphe at either end of the Champs Elysées, and past the Arc de Triomphe, off in the distance, the immense Grand Arch of La Défense, the high-rise business center west of the suburb of Neuilly.

And those are only what can be seen from street level. From higher up the views become breathtaking. For a fee, one

Soaring over the skyline of the Right Bank, the magnificent white Byzantine-inspired domes of Sacré Coeur are visible from almost anywhere in Paris, much like the Eiffel Tower at the other end of the city.

can to climb the stairs to the top of the towers of Notre Dame, or ride the elevator up the Eiffel Tower; but it costs nothing to take the escalator that runs up the outside of the Pompidou Center to the top floor, where you can also look out over all Paris, or to climb the stairs to Sacré Coeur to what may be the very best view of the city spread out below.

In the end, however, no one has seen Paris who has not also looked at it from the riverside, on foot and by boat, following the Seine as it runs its curving course through the city, up from the Eiffel Tower, past the Île de la Cité and the Île St. Louis, and down again past Notre Dame, meeting the Parisians—human, avian, and otherwise—who live on the river.

Finally, there are the parks, most of them elegant, all of them exquisite. At the edge of the city are the former royal hunting grounds: the 2,200-acre (889ha) Bois de Boulogne to the west and the slightly smaller, slightly less famous Bois de Vincennes in the east. Both are lavishly equipped for recreation. The Bois de Boulogne has Longchamps race track, and the famous children's park, the Jardin d'Acclimation; the Bois de Vincennes has a large, modern zoo.

In the center of the city are the former royal gardens, the Tuileries on the Right Bank and the Luxembourg Gardens and *Jardin des Plantes* on the Left. The Tuileries, running from the Louvre to the Place de la Concorde, is a formal garden built over time by French Royals from Catherine de Medicis in 1563 to Louis XIV in 1664. The Jardin du Luxembourg, now the home of the French Senate, is a lovely park with tree-lined walks, formal gardens, and a fountain in which the children of Paris sail model boats. The Jardin des Plantes is the botanical garden of Paris, begun as an herbiary by Louis XIII in 1626 and built up by his successors. A menagerie was added after the Revolution, and the park now houses France's Institute of Natural History.

Not every park in Paris, however, is a centuries-old former royal garden or hunting preserve. High over the northeast of Paris is the splendid Parc des Buttes-Chaumont, created by Haussman for Napoleon III in the 1860s for the Exposition Universelle of 1870. It was an ugly and unsavory stretch of rock quarries and garbage dumps; it became a masterpiece of landscaping, with grottos and watercourses, a music kiosk, and a 100-foot (30m)-high island crowned with a replica of a Roman temple.

And north and east of the Buttes-Chaumont, in the farthest corner of Paris, is the astonishing new Parc de la Villette, one of the most amazing civic enterprises since the Aztec emperors built the floating gardens of Xochimilco. It was intentionally created on the site of the city's old slaughterhouses and the surrounding meatpacking district, carved out of the living city for the use and delight of its people. With performance spaces large and small, fountains throughout, unusual and breathtaking enclosed gardens, and playgrounds for children of different ages, it is a much-loved and much-used center of activity. On weekends, the playgrounds have lines of children waiting to get in; the concert halls and other performance spaces are filled season in and season out; and amateur bands give pass-the-hat concerts in spaces like a miniature concrete amphitheater in the Jardin de Bambou.

The Living City

You don't have to trek to the edge of Paris to experience the city's remarkable vitality. The Parc de la Villette is only one example of Paris' ability to live in the present and provide for the future while cherishing the past. Recent decades have seen a fever of redevelopment, much of it at the initiative of Georges Pompidou and, more significantly, François Mitterrand, presidents of France from 1969 to 1974 and 1981 to 1995, respectively. Indeed, Mitterrand has been credited with changing the face of Paris more than anyone since Haussmann, an assessment that has not necessarily been meant as a compliment.

On the whole, the more drastic changes—especially those that affect the skyline—have been at the edges of the city. Those at the center have been more subtle, which has nonetheless failed to protect them from criticism. The first of the major redevelopments, starting in the 1960s, was in Montparnasse, deep in the Left Bank. The Montparnasse complex includes Paris' first high-rise, the Tour Montparnasse, an undistinguished office tower erected by a city not yet skilled at modernization.

Then came the Centre National d'Art et de Culture—Georges Pompidou. In the heart of the Marais, within sight of Notre Dame, the city built a scandalously modern home for its new National Museum of Modern Art.

Among the more controversial of Mitterrand's *grands projets* was the reconstruction of the Louvre, including a new below-ground entrance hall crowned by a street-level glass pyramid designed in 1981 by architect I.M. Pei.

The biggest project of all was the creation, begun in 1964, of an entire high-rise town, La Défense, two miles west of Paris, past the pleasant suburb of Neuilly. The Grand Arch de la Défense, completed in 1989, is a 320-foot (100m)-high hollow cube set at the far end of La Défense, visible from the center of Paris at the end of the long, straight vista that runs from the Place de la Concorde down the Champs Elysées to the Arche de Triomphe.

None of Mitterrand's projects drew more ire than the Opéra Bastille, opened in 1989. Derided as soulless at best, it is resented by many for being more prominent at the Place de la Bastille than the Colonne de Juillet.

Finally, deep in the Left Bank stands the Bibliothèque National, its four book-shaped glass towers and the immense

The French have as many names for bread as the peoples of the frozen North have for snow: the narrow tartine, the heftier baguette, the Savoyard. There's even one bread known (for reasons no one remembers) as a "batarde"—a bastard.

complex beneath them contain every book and periodical ever published in France.

All these new creations are an expression of Paris' timeless vitality, yet they are not its essence. What holds old and new together and makes Paris *Paris*—beyond its rich history, its culture, its sensuality—are the Parisians themselves. It is Parisian lovers who stroll in the evenings along the banks of the Seine, watching—and being watched by—the tourists in the boats. It is Parisians, too, who patronize the bird market on the quai on the Right Bank, where fowl of every sort, from the tiniest bright canaries to brown turkeys are sold. And it is Parisians who are in and out of the *boulangeries* and the *fromageries* morning and afternoon, carrying their cheeses and *baguettes* home in the baskets of their bicycles.

They are a cosmopolitan lot, the Parisians, descended not only from the ancient European tribes but from the peoples of nearly every quarter of the globe. There are ethnic neighborhoods, like the Jewish section in the Marais near the Pompidou Center, where kosher restaurants and butchers are mixed among the local art galleries and art supply stores. And in addition to its hundreds of bistros serving classic French cuisine, Paris contains scores of

Thai, Vietnamese, Indian, Japanese, and Chinese restaurants, and others still that serve Ethiopian or Greek food. Women, men, and children in traditional African garb ride the Métro alongside people in business suits.

The city's largest minority, its North African population, is represented by couscous restaurants and *halal* butchers (selling meat slaughtered according to Islamic law) in every quarter—and by major institutions as well, which are integrated into the life of the city. Built in the 1920s, the exquisite Paris Mosque on the Left Bank is both a house of worship for Muslims and a sightseeing attraction like the city's churches; it serves an exquisite tea every afternoon except Friday. And the nearby Institut du Monde Arabe on the Left Bank, with its extraordinary wall of iris windows, contains the largest collection of Arab lore outside the Arab world.

Thus, the story of the city that was born two millennia ago on an island in the Seine continues. Here, as perhaps nowhere else in the world, the beauty of the ages inspires without inhibiting, and Paris will enter the twenty-first century as it has entered every century for two thousand years: a city of yesterday, a city of today, a city of tomorrow.

All across Paris, sights like these African drums for sale at the flea market at Porte de Clignancourt are pleasing reminders of the new multi-ethnic vibrancy of this ancient metropolis.

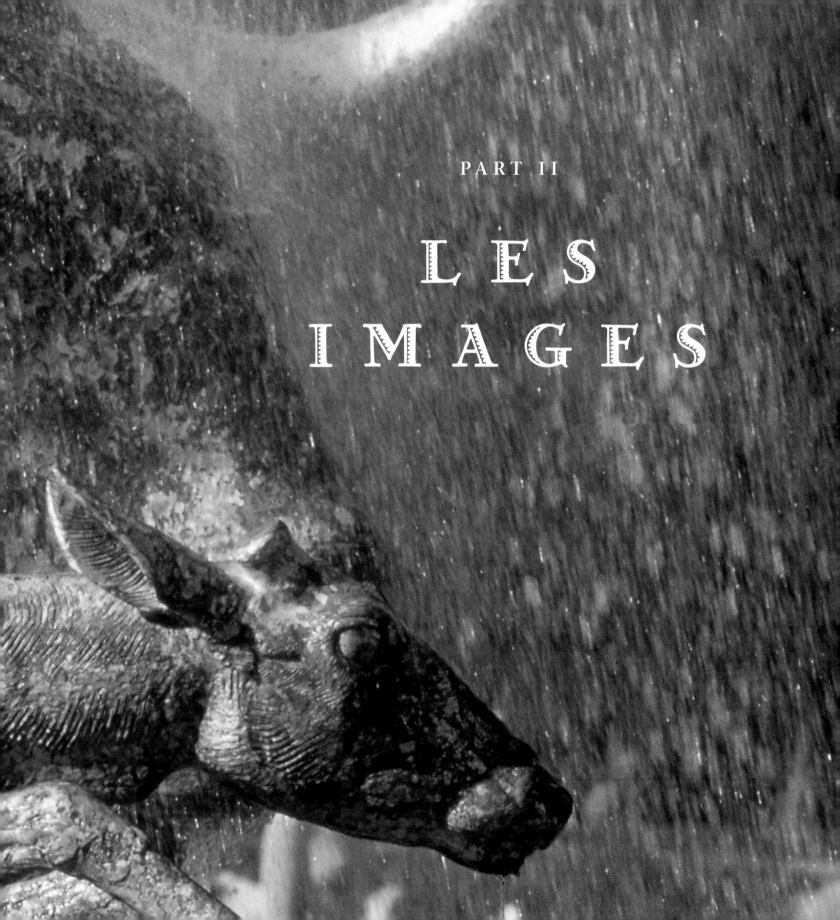

PART II

LES
IMAGES

PAGES 34–35: **The squares and plazas of Paris come in every size, from the monumental to the intimate. The modern Trocadero Garden, created in Art Deco style for the Exposition Universelle of 1937, is one of the monumental sort.**

LEFT: **A sign marks the entrance to a bar in the Marais. For generations, the area was the heart of the city's Jewish community and still has synagogues and kosher butcher shops scattered among the art supply stores that serve students of the massive Pompidou art center.**

ABOVE: **Paris' most expensive antiques—and some of its most glorious desserts—can be found in the shops and cafés that line the arcades at the enchanting Place des Vosges. These aristocratic mansions, built in the seventeenth century, were home then and later to nobility and writers such as Madame de Sévigné and Victor Hugo.**

LEFT: Two empty chairs at a sidewalk café invite a pair of shoppers to take a momentary break over coffee or wine—or perhaps the chairs are waiting for a lovers' rendezvous.

OPPOSITE: If a tourist asks, *"Ou se trouve Montmartre?"* ("Where is Montmartre?"), a Parisian smiles and says, *"Montez, montez, montez!"* ("Climb, climb, climb!"). The reward for the intrepid traveler is a stunning view of all Paris, spread out below like a gift.

OPPOSITE: **Montmartre at night, with the spectral dome of Sacré Coeur hovering over its skyline. Paris is a night town; when the sun sets, the lights come on— and stay on. The bistros of Montmartre—and of most other quarters in the heart of the city—serve dinner until eleven; the cabarets are open into the wee hours.**

RIGHT: **Rarely are the streets of Paris this empty, even late into the night. Perhaps more than any other city in the world, Paris is a pedestrian's pleasure at any time of day.**

A serene oasis in a high-energy city: the Île St. Louis, the tiny island a few yards east of the Île de la Cité, is a sedate and elegant residential neighborhood. Its cafés offer more English-style high teas and deluxe ice cream than wine and night life; Notre Dame is a five-minute walk away.

LEFT: **More tourists visit Paris than come to any other city in the world, making it easy to forget that it is also home to hundreds of thousands of families—and tens of thousands of cats.**

ABOVE: **Parisians prefer to buy their food fresh and tend to shop every day, rain or shine.**

The Pont au Change crosses
the Seine from the Right Bank
to the Palais de Justice on the
Île de la Cité; behind the
bridge is the Conciergerie,
which served as a prison during
the Revolution, and its
fourteenth-century clock
tower, the Tour de l'Horloge.

Directly across the Seine from the Eiffel Tower—built for the 1899 Exposition—is the Art Deco Palais de Chaillot,

built for the 1937 Exposition Universelle, its sweeping curves visible here behind the fountains of its Trocadero Garden.

Like many of Paris' monuments, the fountains and garden are lit at night to provide a different—and dazzling—vision.

ABOVE: **Even in the historical potpourri of the Marais, the Hôtel Carnavalet stands out. Its oldest parts date to the sixteenth century, it's newest sections to the nineteenth. Now a museum, the building and its contents display and exemplify Paris' rich history.**

OPPOSITE: **Reflections on the Seine at sunset, closing out another day and preparing the city for the captivating beauty that takes over at night as Paris truly becomes the City of Light.**

In the brilliant afternoon sun, a Parisian reads a newspaper at the edge of the Seine near the Louvre.
Parisian traffic can be hellish, but it would be even worse if the thousands who cycle were also driving.

The quais along the Seine in the Latin Quarter and the neighboring Sixth Arrondissement are lined with
used book stands selling printed matter of every kind, from valuable first editions to paperback
French translations of 1950s American detective novels.

The Pont des Arts is the only pedestrian-only bridge in central Paris, crossing the Seine at the foot of the Île de la Cité, from the Louvre on the right bank to the Institut de France and the Museum of the Paris Mint on the left. Just east of the bridge, on the tip of the Île de la Cité, is the delightful square du Vert-Galant, an oasis of green on an island chock-full of ancient buildings.

Commissioned by Henri IV in 1604, the Pont Neuf, or "new bridge," is actually the oldest spanning the Seine.

Here, it has been adorned with flowers to celebrate the arrival of spring.

A whimsical wall painting
covers both corners of a
building in the quiet
residential northeast of Paris.

A Parisian walks his dog along
the Seine. The residents of this
city don't just take their dogs
for walks; they bring them
along in the Métro, to the cafés,
and in little baskets on the
handlebars of their bicycles.

LEFT: The fountain in the Place Igor Stravinsky—like the Pompidou Center next door—is an exception to the stone-gray and tree-green that are the predominant colors of Paris. The whimsical moving figures sculpted by Jean Tinguely and Niki de Saint-Phalle in 1983 delight Parisians and tourists alike.

ABOVE: In front of the Pompidou Center, an immense plaza—in a shallow bowl shaped almost like an amphitheater—is host every day and into the evening to street singers, mimes, sword-swallowers, caricaturists, and other artists and performers.

More formal than the
Luxembourg Gardens across the
Seine, the Tuileries nevertheless
draws its share of playful
children to sail model boats
in its pool...

...or ride its carousel. Almost every park in Paris has at least one carousel, as do many plazas, including—incongruously—the open spaces in front of the city's most dignified monuments.

ABOVE: **Part of Baron Haussmann's massive reconstruction of Paris, the Place de la Concorde is dominated by this immense fountain, as well as the 3,300-year-old obelisk that was sent from Egypt in 1833.**

RIGHT: **The Belle Epoque Pont Alexandre III forms part of the vista that runs from the Petit Palais—of the same period—to the domed Baroque Les Invalides, which now houses Napoleon's tomb and a museum of arms.**

✧

OPPOSITE: **The ceiling of the Arc de Triomphe. The arch stands in the Place Charles de Gaulle, from which twelve avenues radiate outward—and which can only be crossed through underground tunnels.**

BELOW: **The graceful wrought iron that characterizes so many of Paris' nineteenth-century doorways, windows, and balconies provides a sense of timeless elegance to even the most mundane spaces.**

PAGES 64–65: **Looking westward along the Seine at everyone's vision of Paris: the Île St. Louis (right) and Notre Dame (left) at night.**

Every building in Paris is within one-third of a mile (500m) of a Métro station. The Paris Métro, opened in 1900, now has 368 stations and transports six million passengers per day, most of them Parisians or residents of the nearby suburbs.

Many of the oldest Métro stations are still graced with their original entranceway signs, designed by
sculptor Hector Guimard around the turn of the century.

Off the Quai St. Michel in the
Latin Quarter, a tangled warren
of pedestrian-only streets
evokes the Paris of an earlier
age—even as the dozens of
North African couscous and
Greek souvlaki restaurants
fill the area, signifying an
ever-changing culture.

"Taxi!" Like most subway systems around the world, the Paris Métro shuts down around 1:00 A.M. Although most of the city remains safe for walking well into the early morning hours, taxis offer the quickest way to get around Paris after midnight.

ABOVE: **A vintage sign outside a Paris wine bar. The prices have gone up since this was painted.**

BELOW: **Wine and its divinity: A mask of Dionysios, the ancient Greek god of the vine, hangs over a corner in the old Marais quarter.**

ABOVE: **Paris has generated artistic and intellectual ferment and creativity for generations; it was here, in the cafés along the Boulevard St. Germain, on the west side of the Boulevard St. Michel, that Existentialism came to its full flowering after World War II.**

THESE PAGES: **Two gothic visions at Notre Dame: inside, the soaring vaulted ceiling (opposite) attests to the builders' genius;** **while outside (above), one of the cathedrals' dozens of gargoyles gazes out over the Paris skyline.**

A tree-lined quay provides a pleasant place for a stroll along the bank of the Seine,

one of many picturesque promenades in pedestrian-friendly Paris.

BELOW: **Relaxing by the Seine on a sunny summer afternoon, a student takes a few moments to enjoy the fine weather.**

Paris has hundreds of
flower shops and dozens of
flower markets, the largest
on the Île de la Cité, not far
from Notre Dame; this one is
on the Left Bank, along
the Boulevard Raspail.

Parisians take their cheese very seriously. At supermarkets or *fromageries*, there are myriad varieties, each with its
own subtle distinction. Here a vendor inspects his Camemberts.

Hundreds of Paris' distinguished dead rest in the Cimetière du Père Lachaise. Pictured here, the columbarium
holds the ashes of some of the city's better-known former residents—including the American dancer Isadora Duncan.
Among those buried here are writers Marcel Proust, Oscar Wilde, Colette, and Gertrude Stein; actors Sarah Bernhardt and
Simone Signoret, the latter buried with her husband, singer-actor Yves Montand; Paris' "little sparrow," singer Edith Piaf;
and American rock idol Jim Morrison.

On the Île de la Cité, a study
in contrasts: the grim, gray
Conciergerie of the Palais de
Justice and its representatives,
the Paris police; and one of
the many flower stands of the
island's *marche des fleurs*.

By day, the entrance to the Louvre, by night a place of enchantment: the fountains at architect I.M. Pei's glass pyramid.

One of the hundreds of Greek and Roman antiquities in the world's greatest art museum. The Louvre's miles of corridors are so long and
so filled with the paintings and sculptures of the ages that it would take years to examine them all.

The Belle Epoque railroad station on the Seine, the Gare d'Orsay, had outlived its usefulness as a transport hub by mid-century. In 1986, Paris' municipal government turned it into the Musée d'Orsay, the new home of the city's extensive collection of impressionist art.

Another Paris contrast: the whimsical, folk-influenced 1964 painting by the Russian-Jewish artist Marc Chagall
on the ceiling of the luxuriant, formal, nineteenth century Paris Opera House.

LEFT: The stained glass windows of Ste. Chapelle, the oldest in Paris, were commissioned
in the fourteenth century by Louis IX, St. Louis.

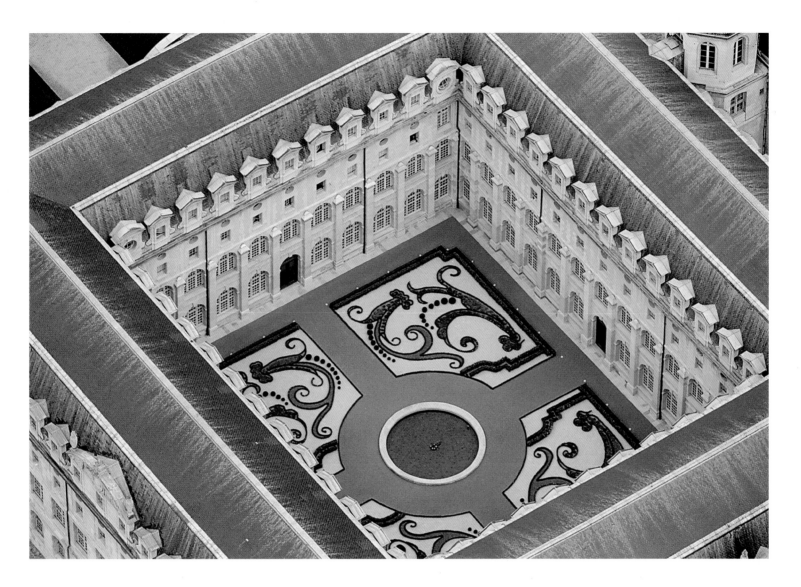

ABOVE: **The Val de Grace complex, seen here from the air, was built in the seventeenth century as a church and home for the Benedictine religious community. It was turned into a military hospital after the Revolution.**

ABOVE: Built in the 1950s by the French government, the Paris Mosque was created with input from North African Muslims to ensure its authenticity. It can hold five hundred worshipers. Non-Muslims are welcome at its café, which serves tea and North African delicacies.

OPPOSITE: Near the Mosque, a labyrinthine walkway is the focal point of an exquisite garden.

OPPOSITE: **The Grand Arch of La Défense, the massive business complex outside Paris, seen from underneath, with the Teflon, steel, and glass sculpture "Clouds" by Peter Rice in the foreground.**

ABOVE: **Water cascades over the colorful mosaic floor of a fountain in a plaza among the skyscrapers of La Défense.**

Large department stores began to appear in Paris late in the last century. This is the 1912 cupola of the Galeries Lafayette, perhaps the grandest of them all.

The amazing iron construction of the Eiffel Tower allows for striking views from any perspective. While scenic views of the landmark towering above the city remain a postcard standard, the view looking up from beneath the enormous structure is even more impressive.

LEFT: **The sculptor Auguste Rodin lived in this Left Bank house for the last nine years of his life; on his death, he bequeathed his work to the French government, which turned the house into a museum celebrating his life and art.**

OPPOSITE: **The gardens of the Forum des Halles, the mall complex built between 1979 and 1988 on the site of Paris' ancient central food market. In the distance is the late Renaissance-Gothic St. Eustache Church, built in the seventeenth century in a style that was already old-fashioned.**

PAGE 96: **The silhouettes of Butte Montmarte and Sacré Coeur glow in the fading light outside the window of a Parisian home. Stunning views and beautiful cityscapes are things that not even lifelong residents take for granted.**

PHOTO CREDITS

Every effort has been made to ascertain and correctly credit the copyright holders and/or owners for all images appearing in this book. The publisher will correct mistaken credits and include any omitted credits in all future editions.

Corbis: p. 51; ©Yann Arthus-Bertrand: pp. 4–5, 85, 86–87; ©Dave Bartruff: pp. 6, 45 right, 66; ©Morton Beebe: pp. 37, 79; ©Owen Franken: pp. 53, 70 left, 77, 86 left; ©Marc Garanger: pp. 88–89; ©Philip Gould: p. 70 right;

©Richard Hamilton-Smith: pp. 44–45; ©Robert Holmes: pp. 13, 54, 57 right, 71, 74, 78, 89 right; ©Wolfgang Kaehler: pp. 56–57; ©Richard List: p. 55; ©Ludovic Maisant: p. 93

©John Elk III: pp. 10–11, 21, 60–61

FPG International/©David A. Barnes: pp. 33, 58; ©Walter Bibikow: pp. 64–65; ©Ron Chapple: p. 18; ©Tom Craig: pp. 46, 48; ©Robert Cundy: p. 15; ©Bill Deering: p. 76; ©Richard Laird: pp. 62, 69; ©Mike Malyszko: p.1; ©Ken Ross: p. 39; ©David Sacks: p. 23; ©Stephen Simpson: pp. 38, 92;

©Richard H. Smith: pp. 7, 82; ©Arthur Tilley: pp. 52, 59; ©Toyohiro Yamada: pp. 22, 83

©Michael Halberstadt: p. 72

©Robert Holmes: pp. 24, 25, 36, 50

©Carol Kitman: p. 63

Leo de Wys/©Bas Van Beek: p. 29; ©Arthur Hustwitt: p. 73

©Craig Lovell: pp. 17, 47, 91

©Richard Nowitz: p. 68

©Allan A. Philiba: pp. 30, 32, 90

Photo Network/©Chad Ehlers: p. 40

Photophile/©Alex Bartel: p. 27

©Andrea Pistolesi: pp. 2–3, 34–35, 42–43, 53, 60 left, 67, 84, 94

Positive Images/©Patricia J. Bruno: p. 14

©Carl Purcell: p. 81

©H. Armstrong Roberts: p. 41

©David Sailors: p. 80

Scope: p. 49; ©Chris Cheadle: pp. 9

Summer Productions/©Ted Wood: p. 75